MW00528323

THE POWER OF PERSONAL LEADERSHIP

Building Your Future One Choice at a Time

DANNY LANIER

The Power of Personal Leadership: Building Your Future One Choice at a Time

Published by Wheatmark®
610 East Delano Street, Suite 104
Tucson, Arizona 85705 U.S.A.
www.wheatmark.com

International Standard Book Number: 978-1-60494-041-1
(hardcover)
International Standard Book Number: 978-1-58736-071-8
(paperback)

Library of Congress Control Number: 2007940105

CONTENTS

ACKNOWLEDGMENTS

Writing a book takes far more effort than meets the eye. The road between having an idea and writing a book can be long and winding. Like any journey, you may have to seek guidance from others along the way. My commitment to getting this book done was very strong, but I was equally inspired by those who cheered me on and provided good insight. My thanks go out to a lot of people, and while I run the risk of overlooking someone, I offer the following summary of those who come to mind.

I thank my wife, Rose, for having patience with me and giving me the space and support that I needed to get this project done. Thanks to Marilyn Pincus, who assisted me with my first book and insisted that there was at least one more book left in me. I would also like to thank Dennis Carey, Gracie Coleman, and Frank D'Amelio for their willingness to endorse my first book and for giving me encouragement on this one.

I thank Dr. Benjamin Newhouse, former dean of the College of Business and Information Science at Tuskegee University, for persuading me to join the Tuskegee University faculty. The university environment has provided an additional incentive to complete this work as a way of giving back to the community through sharing of ideas and lessons learned over three decades.

Thanks to Dr. Stuart Youngblood, professor of management at Texas Christian University; Dr. Leo T. Upchurch, professor of economics at Tuskegee University; Randolph Stratford; and JaQuile Miller for providing feedback on my manuscript. Your time, effort, and valuable feedback were greatly appreciated.

Thanks to Dr. Seth Anderson, professor of finance at Tuskegee University, for sharing his experience with various publishers and providing me a recommendation for publishing services.

Finally, I would like to thank all the people in my personal life and my professional life that have shared ideas or provided good leadership examples for this book. You made an impact on me, and I hope that I have accurately told your stories. You are an important part of my memories. I learned a lot from each of you.

INTRODUCTION

Most leadership books deal with the challenges of leading others. This book deals with one of the most critical challenges of all: leading oneself. It is nearly impossible to lead others until you have learned how to lead yourself. What I have learned over time is that success is as much about who you become as a person as what you achieve. When we are young, we get accustomed to others making choices on our behalf. The rationale for this is that we let those with more knowledge and experience make the important calls. As we get older and wiser, there comes a time when we should begin to make our own decisions and choose our own direction. We should decide what type of person we want to become and what we wish to achieve. It takes courage to make that transition, but successful people do it all the time. This is when you begin to become your own person. By leading yourself, you become your own person. Only then can you effectively lead others. Personal leadership is choosing to own your future and holding yourself accountable for the choices you make and their consequences.

There is a process that people go through to transform themselves and become effective self-leaders. The process begins with a decision to accept ownership for designing your future. This first step is critical, because until you accept ownership for your future, you are leaving it to others to decide. The second step is understanding yourself and the world around you to determine where you fit in. The third step is creating a personal vision of who you want to be and what you want to accomplish. Your vision and values will guide your life choices. The fourth step is laying a solid foundation for your plan by defining your values, character, and identity. The fifth step is choosing the right priorities based on your vision and goals. For example, if good health and financial security are important to you, then your priorities should reflect that. The next two steps are embracing change and overcoming adversity. Change and adversity are two great learning opportunities that you will face throughout your life. You can learn and grow if you embrace change and learn from the challenges and setbacks in life. Since no one succeeds alone, the next two steps are critical. Building relationships and maximizing synergy allow you to expand your influence. Each person has unique talents, and great leaders learn how to bring them together and accomplish more than they could ever accomplish alone. The last step, giving back, may be the most rewarding. This gives our lives meaning and makes all of the other steps seem worthwhile.

This book describes the process of transforming yourself to become an effective person. It reveals the power of personal leadership. It explains that you are in charge of yourself, and that the choices you make will define your future. It was written primarily for young adults seeking to become more effective in their personal and professional lives. It will also benefit those approaching the middle of their careers who feel compelled to make a change. I invite you to take the journey with me as I describe this transformation process.

1

ACCEPTING OWNERSHIP

It is easy to get comfortable with deferring your life decisions to other people. Some people believe that this keeps them from being held accountable if things don't work out. Successful people make their own decisions after consulting with others in whom they have confidence. They know themselves, their capabilities, and what they want out of life. Oprah Winfrey could have let the opinions of her boss at a television station in Baltimore limit her future, but instead she accepted ownership of her future and began making choices consistent with what she wanted to become. She took a job in Chicago as a talk show host and has been influencing lives ever since.

I was playing a round of golf with Eric Snow of the Cleveland Cavaliers when he shared the following story with me. While he was playing for an NBA team on the West Coast, his coach would not give him much playing time. He believed that with more playing time he would be able to prove himself. He had a choice between accepting his coach's opinion or seeking playing opportunities elsewhere. Eric demonstrated personal leadership by requesting a trade to Philadelphia. He not only received more playing time there, he became a starter and played a significant role on a winning team. After playing there for a few years, he moved to the Cleveland Cavaliers, where he just finished playing in the NBA Finals. Sometimes you have to create situations where your talents can be exposed.

The moment of truth for me came in 1982, when I was being recruited for a staff position by Jack Heck, an executive at AT&T. Jack explained to me that he needed someone with my background to fill a key position on his staff and why the exposure would be good for my career. After the interview, he said that he wanted me to think about my answer before I gave it, because he didn't want anybody on his staff who didn't want to be there. This was a major decision that involved relocating my family from Atlanta to New Jersey, and I had already turned the job down once. What Jack was doing was forcing me to be accountable for my decision. I would not be able to say he made me do it. I decided to take the position, knowing that the decision would be mine alone and I would have to live with the consequences.

Even though Jack had recruited me, he did not make the transition easy. I guess I got on his bad side right away when I didn't have lunch with him and the other staff members. He had a practice of having lunch with his staff to get to know them and get updates on any hot topics. No one told me about the practice, so I went out to lunch with a friend. When I returned, a coworker said that Jack was upset with me for not showing up at lunch. When I did attend lunch with him, he said I didn't talk enough. He also challenged me at every turn to see if I was learning my job. You didn't hang around Jack if you were not prepared. I took it as a personal challenge to not be intimidated by him and to prove my worth. Jack was transferred after six months, but he told me before he left that I was doing a good job. The decision to transfer to New Jersey had turned out to be a good one.

When I reflect on that decision today, I realize what a defining moment it was. It launched a series of career moves and promotions that almost certainly would not have happened had I not taken that position. There was risk and inconvenience involved, but the rewards were far greater. What I learned from the experience is that you have to know yourself, your capabilities, and what you want out of life. No one knows your heart and aspirations better than you do. When it is time to step up to the plate, you have to do it (make your own choices). Otherwise, you will limit your career.

When I left Atlanta for New Jersey in 1982, most of my peers questioned my judgment, since it was a lateral move with no promise of a promotion. What I was promised was good exposure, a great learning opportunity, and a chance to demonstrate my abilities in a different environment. Most people would have expected more to make such a move, but I could see the possibilities and was willing to take the risk. I believe that few great things are achieved without some risk. Otherwise, everyone would be doing great things. By the way, many of the people who told me that I was crazy for going to New Jersey still had the same jobs when I retired in 1999. Yes, success takes talent, but it also takes vision, courage, and a willingness to change.

You probably know people who are very talented, but because of fear, they never use their talents to elevate themselves. Some people like to blame circumstances and other people for their lack of success. When they see someone who is doing well, they attribute it to luck. Sometimes people write themselves off because they did not achieve an *A* average or could not qualify for a top-tier college. Getting *A*s and graduating from a prestigious college can definitely give you a short-term advantage, but as I tell my students at Tuskegee, in the long run, it is effectiveness that really counts. After you have been out of school for a few years, you will be measured more by your effectiveness than where you went to school or your grade point average. A recent poll of 234 people by the *Memphis Business Chronicle* on June 13, 2007, showed that 66 percent of the respondents believe that where you went to college matters less over time. Also, according to Dr. Thomas J. Stanley, author of *The Millionaire Mind* (2000), the top three success factors cited in a survey of 733 millionaires were honesty, discipline, and getting along with people. Leadership qualities ranked seventh, while attending a top-tier college ranked twenty-third out of thirty.

Taking ownership of your life gives you the freedom to explore options without feeling like you have to stay true to the script that someone else has written for you. Know that you have a right to choose your own script and use your unique talents to make an impact in the world. You can decide if you are satisfied with where you are in life, and if you are, let that be your decision. If you are not, you now know that you can change yourself and the things around you without permission. This is what I mean by taking ownership.

Another reason why taking ownership of your future is so important is that no one educational experience can prepare you for life. Learning is a lifelong process that requires your personal leadership. No one can do it for you, because experience and reflection are a big part of the learning process. You have to pro-actively harness all of the experiences, exposure, and challenges that life throws your way and use them to transform yourself into the person you want to be. You are the director, producer, script writer, and actor all wrapped into one.

Practice Accepting Ownership

Accepting ownership of your choices in your personal and professional life is a critical first step to building the future that you desire. List five key choices in each area listed below for which you are willing to hold yourself personally accountable.

Personal Choices:

1.

2.

3.

4.

5.

Professional Choices:

1.

2.

3.

4.

5.

2

SEEKING UNDERSTANDING

Once you have taken ownership of your personal and professional lives, you must seek understanding of yourself and the world around you. Each of us is born with some God-given talents. Our challenge is to figure out what those talents are, develop them, and use them to make a contribution to society. To determine how your talents can be used requires an understanding of the world around you. Determine where there is a need for your talents, and opportunities will follow. Some people reach this level of understanding early in life, while others arrive there much later. Unfortunately, some never figure it out.

According to Peter Drucker, success comes to those who know their strengths, their values, and how they best perform. In his book *Management Challenges for the 21st Century* (1999), Drucker outlines how people differ in their methods of learning and performing. He states that you must not only learn these things about yourself, but you should learn them about your peers, your boss, and your team. With this knowledge you are better able to maximize each person's contribution.

Most companies have standard educational requirements that must be met to get an opportunity. Whether you are planning to own your own business or become a doctor, lawyer, or politician, a standard level of knowledge will always be required. Once you have met that standard, you can decide how much additional knowledge you will need based on your aspirations. Not all the knowledge you will gain comes from formal education. People learn from life experiences, listening, reading, and observing. Talk show host Larry King never attended college, but he was a curious person who learned from others. He knew that his passion was in broadcasting, and he learned how to be a professional through experience and observing others around him.

Traveling to other countries or a different region of this country is another way to expand your knowledge and perspective. There is so much to learn about how other people live, how they view the world, and what their priorities are. I remember traveling to South America and seeing the pride that people in that region have in their history and the products they produce. When I traveled to Asia, it was amazing to see how generations of people worked on temples, statues, and buildings that would not be completed in their lifetime. They had a vision of a better future for their children. We in this country are blessed with access to so many resources that I think sometimes we take it all for granted. We all need to make life better for the next generation.

One of my other observations while traveling abroad was that people generally speak two or more languages. Speaking a second or third language opens up many options, since it allows you to communicate with people in their native language. This facilitates learning and also helps build relationships. People in other countries are more receptive when you can speak their language or at least say a few words. Most of my international travel came toward the end of my career, and I had to use translators whenever I traveled to Latin America or China. I have continued to travel since retiring from corporate America, and I continue to learn. However, I would strongly recommend learning a second language as early as possible. I believe that companies will be expecting employees to do much more international travel in the future. Also, with the world becoming smaller due to improved communication and increased airline travel, you may want to learn a new language just to facilitate your own business or enhance your personal travel experience.

Many people learn by reflecting on their experiences. As you are exposed to different situations, you may not handle all of them in the best way the first time. By reflecting on your experiences, you will be able to see what worked well and where there are opportunities for improvement. People who don't reflect on their experiences are likely to make the same mistakes again. Mistakes are a part of self-development only if you learn from them. That is how most people grow into their jobs. Often people are selected for jobs not because they meet every single requirement but because they have the potential to develop the knowledge and skills that are required.

Many people struggle with money issues early in life. My wife and I were no exception. We married very young and made many of the typical mistakes that most inexperienced people make. We spent more than we were making and ran up quite a bit of debt. However, we learned from those mistakes and became better money managers as a result. We were fortunate to learn those lessons early in life, before we reached higher income levels and had much more responsibility. I encourage you to take a look at how well you manage your finances. If you have made some mistakes in the past, just remember that mistakes are a part of the learning process. Study your financial habits and make changes that will prevent similar mistakes in the future.

This type of learning shapes every aspect of our lives. We learn how to take better care of our health, our relationships, our business, and our careers by learning from mistakes we make along the way. When we are young, we sometimes neglect our health and our relationships in pursuit of a career or hobby. We fail to balance our lives until something goes wrong or breaks down. I admit to neglecting my health during much of my career. Fortunately, I didn't have any major problems, but I discovered that I have hypertension. It has changed my lifestyle significantly. No one can teach you how to prepare for every possible life situation. You will have your own unique challenges. That is why you will have to lead your own development process. You must exercise personal leadership in every area of your life.

When you take a new job, no one expects you to know everything the first day. If you do, you won't grow very much in that job. Each assignment should expose you to something new, challenge you to learn new skills, and position you for future growth. Anything less and you are just spinning your wheels. Even if a new job pays more than your current one, it may not be the right one for you. I turned down two promotions late in my career because the jobs were outside of my stated career path. Sure, I could have used the extra income, but it may have taken me out of the position to obtain a future job in my chosen field. My goal was to be a force within the financial community and support the careers of those who had contributed so much to mine.

You should read at least three books a year by respected people in your profession and seek time with people who are already doing what you want to do. Your circumstances will likely be different, but you can learn some of the keys to success and the major pitfalls that you should avoid. You will learn that success requires much more than just technical skills. It also requires good character, leadership skills, people skills, and the ability to deal with change and adversity.

Understanding your strengths and weaknesses helps you make better career choices. According to Emory Mulling, author of *The Mulling Factor* (2002), you are misemployed if your boss, your work, or your environment is out of sync with your personality. Getting into the right situation is your responsibility. This is the main reason for seeking to understand yourself and the world around you before you choose a new job or new career. If you have already chosen a career, make sure you are in the right job to fit your strengths and personality. The sooner you make this assessment the quicker you will gain traction and see positive results.

Jackie Moore, a former coworker, had good accounting skills, but her personality was that of a salesper-
son. As a result, she found that people in accounting
didn't take her as seriously as she had hoped. After a
few years in accounting, a friend suggested that she
try sales. After doing some research, Jackie left the
accounting profession and became a successful real
estate agent. My wife and I used her services on two
occasions as we relocated to and from Atlanta. Jackie
said she has never been happier. She had exercised
personal leadership to put herself in a winning situation. Jackie is now retired and lives in Florida with
her husband.

Jim Smith, a former engineer with Western Electric,
moved to Atlanta in 1976, after his job was transferred
there from Buffalo. Once he got settled in, he decided
that Atlanta would be his home and he never wanted
to relocate again. His family loved it, he loved it, and
things were going well with his job. However, in an
effort to further his career, Jim left engineering and
moved to finance. His assignment in finance was as
district manager of payroll. Things went well for a
while, but as the company changed, he was faced
with the possibility of having to move his family
again. He left the company and became vice president
of operations for TriNet Corporation, a payroll and
benefits provider in Reno, Nevada. I am sure when
Jim started his career in Buffalo, New York, he didn't

expect to end up in Reno, Nevada, with a payroll and benefits company. Most careers will have twists and turns, but the people who use personal leadership usually make the right choice for themselves. Jim and his family are happy with where they are today.

Randy Stratford was an accounting manager with Ford, Bacon & Davis in Dallas, Texas, during the 1980s when his company was acquired by an international group. Soon after the acquisition Randy was asked to consider a relocation. He had no interest in relocating, so he used his network to locate a position with Ericsson, a Swedish telecommunications company. He joined Ericsson as assistant controller and was later promoted to controller. Randy had mastered personal leadership and knew the choices he had to make. He knew he had to seek other employment if he wanted to stay in the Dallas area. He used his network to land on his feet with another company. Sometimes people wait too long for their companies to do something for them. By the time they figure out that the company is not planning to do anything, it is usually too late. Randy had a successful career with Ericsson and won the hearts and minds of the people he worked with. He retired in July of 2007 to spend more time with his grandchildren.

These are three examples of individuals who took ownership of their careers and made the choices they had to make to match their strengths with where the opportunities were. As you prepare for your career, keep in mind that opportunities are not always right in front of you. You may have to change what you do or move to another city in order for your career to flourish. Not everyone will agree with your decision, but you have to do what is best for you. Your circumstances and aspirations may be different from those of your friends and colleagues.

Practice Seeking Understanding

Understanding yourself and the world around you helps you to know who you are and how you fit in. List five things that you will do to better understand yourself and the world around you.

To better understand myself, I will:

1.

2.

3.

4.

5.

To better understand the world around me, I will:

1.

2.

3.

4.

5.

3

CREATING A PERSONAL VISION

An understanding of yourself and the world around you is a prerequisite to creating a personal vision. You may have been influenced by your parents, teachers, or friends to pursue a particular lifestyle or profession. While we love to please those close to us, they often do not know our true talents or what is in our heart. Since you are the one who must live with the outcome, it is important that you choose your own path. So many people live to regret not following their dreams, either because they were influenced by others or lacked the confidence to go their own way. Creating a personal vision takes courage, but an understanding of your talents and the world around you will give you the confidence you need to create your personal vision.

Tiger Woods had the ability to excel in several sports; however, after some soul-searching, he chose golf because that was where his heart was. He had talent, a great mentor, and a great determination to learn the game. Tiger became a student of the game and learned about the great players of the past. He studied what made them successful and evaluated his own talents. He then created a vision of where he wanted to position himself in the golf history books. When your head is clear about what you want to do and your heart is in it, the other things come much easier. The choice of profession must be yours and yours alone. Tiger has become one of the best golfers to play the game.

Michael Dell had plans to become a doctor, but because of his love for computers, he chose a different path and formed the Dell Corporation in 1984. Today, Dell is a multibillion-dollar corporation and Michael Dell is one of the richest men in America. He had a combination of vision, talent, desire, courage, and leadership to help him succeed. He may have become an excellent doctor, but by following his heart and talents he is making a great contribution to society.

Fred Smith wrote a term paper about an overnight delivery service while attending Yale. His professor gave him a C on his paper and told him his idea was not practical. Smith took his concept and founded Federal Express in 1973. Had he listened to his professor, he might not have pursued his dream of building an overnight delivery service. Sometimes people will question your vision, but if you are passionate enough and stick with it, good things usually happen. Today FedEx is a leading overnight delivery service.

It was very clear to me when I entered college that my future would be in business, even though a close friend had tried to talk me into engineering. I liked the interaction and growth possibilities that business provided. I envisioned learning a business and leading large groups of people to achieving goals for a company and for themselves. I was intrigued by how businesses developed, implemented strategies, and made adjustments to stay ahead of their competition. It just seemed dynamic to me.

I became interested in accounting during my sophomore year at Tuskegee University. Mobil Corporation, in an effort to increase minority participation in its accounting department, sponsored an expenses-paid trip to New York City for one student from each of ten black colleges. There was an essay contest at each college to determine who would participate. We had to write an essay on what we hoped to learn from a week in the business world and a review of the accounting profession. I won the essay contest at Tuskegee and spent five days in New York with Mobil's financial executives. We looked at different accounting jobs, discussed their requirements, and looked at how the executives lived. When I returned to Tuskegee, I was pretty certain that this was the area of business that I wanted to pursue.

Over the next two summers I had internships with Mobil and GE and learned more about the accounting profession. By the time I graduated, I had received a job offer from both companies. The offer from GE was good, but I accepted the offer from Mobil and entered a supervisory training program in Buffalo, New York. My supervisor, George Swanson, became a good friend and mentor. He taught me the importance of being prepared whenever we had visitors from the home office. Since I was young and inexperienced, he pulled me aside and coached me whenever he saw me doing something that was not good for my career. I eventually left Mobil and started a career with AT&T, but I knew by then that accounting would be my lifelong profession.

My vision was to become a successful financial executive through hard work, continuous learning, compassion for people, and integrity. I wanted people on my team to work hard, but I also wanted them to work smart and look for more effective ways of getting things done. I wanted people around me to have integrity and compassion for the people on their teams. I believed that our reputations for good character were linked. It's important to have people around you who share your vision.

By creating a vision, you know better how to deploy yourself. You know which jobs and relationships are in your best interest and which ones you should avoid. I remember turning down two promotions during my career because I didn't think they fit within my vision. If you don't have a vision, you may find yourself taking jobs for the wrong reasons. I always believed that a job should challenge you, expand your knowledge, and position you for greater responsibility within your chosen field. A temporary increase in pay may not be enough for a dead-end job, which does little to position you for the future.

One of the people I met at company headquarters was Ernie Mackey. Ernie was a bright young man who had come from Ohio to New Jersey for some of the same reasons that I had. He was seeking to broaden his experience, develop some new relationships, and learn more about the business. While Ernie and I did not work very closely due to the timing of our arrivals and departures from headquarters, we became friends and kept in touch. Ernie chose operations over accounting and was held in high regard by top management. However, he chose to go in a different direction and is now vice president of operations at JNET Communications in Atlanta. He exercised personal leadership in deciding what was best for him at that point in his career. Some people did not agree with his decision, but he had the courage to follow his dreams. We play golf occasionally and still talk about career strategies and the importance of personal leadership.

A good friend from my college days is a family physician in Montgomery, Alabama. Dr. William Abernathy is the nephew of Ralph David Abernathy, the civil rights leader. He and I were in the same graduating class. Dr. Abernathy was a fun-loving student, just like most of the people in our circle of friends, but he was on a mission to become a doctor. He told me that he had always enjoyed helping people who needed medical care. He became a commissioned officer in the army right after graduation and later attended the University of Alabama medical school. He established his practice in Montgomery in the late 1970s and is still going strong to this day. I tell this story because he had a vision very early in life and was able to realize it.

Lionel Richie, the legendary singer and songwriter, was another college classmate. He was a business major, but he clearly had a different vision. He played the saxophone in Tuskegee's marching band and became a member of the singing group the Commodores before breaking out on his own. His decision to join the group and delay his college graduation was a display of personal leadership. He knew that he was faced with the opportunity of a lifetime. Lionel completed his degree in 1973. He would later make an even bigger decision to become a solo artist. His vision and passion were two of the most important things contributing to his success. He is a superstar around the globe, but he still has close friends in Tuskegee, Alabama.

Dr. Ben Carson, director of pediatric neurosurgery at Johns Hopkins Hospital, was once called the class dummy by his classmates. He discovered the power of knowledge after his mother made him read two books a week and watch less television. Dr. Carson went from the bottom of his class to the top in a year and a half. He initially wanted to be a missionary doctor but decided he would rather do something that paid more money. He became fascinated by the human brain and decided to become a brain surgeon. He later became famous for separating a set of South African twins who were joined at the head. No one in his class could see the possibilities, but he had a vision of his future.

Each of these individuals started out with a vision of what they wanted to become. They honed their skills and looked for the right partners or the right opportunities. People are much more likely to support you in the pursuit of your dreams if they sense that you have a passion and a plan. A banker wants to see your business plan before he gives you a business loan. A builder wants to know your vision for your home before he builds it. Everything in life is created twice. First it is created mentally, and then it is created physically. Everything begins with a vision.

Practice Creating a Personal Vision

A personal vision defines the type of person you want to be and the things you hope to achieve. Use the space below to write a personal vision. Think deeply about how you would like to be known and remembered as a person, and clearly define the most important things that you want to achieve. Remember, you are writing this for yourself, so you must be committed to what you write.

4

LAYING A SOLID FOUNDATION

People judge you more by what you do than by what you say. This is especially true when there is a significant gap between the two. No matter how great your talent, your character plays a major role in how others perceive you. There have been countless cases in which very talented people of great power and influence have lost jobs, customers, fans, and sponsors because of character flaws. Many athletes, entertainers, businesspeople, and politicians have had their characters questioned.

Pete Rose was banned from baseball because he was suspected of betting on baseball while he was the manager of a team. Several Enron executives pleaded guilty to "cooking the books," which led to the collapse of the company. A former governor of Alabama was recently found guilty of receiving contributions in return for making a key board appointment. The former CEO of WorldCom was convicted of pressuring his CFO to hide expenses and overstate profits. These are just a few of the cases making headlines over the past several years.

When a person makes poor choices they usually affect other people around them like family members, colleagues, investors, or employees. The executives at Enron and WorldCom not only destroyed their own careers, but they also affected the careers of their employees and the wealth of many investors. Their families were also affected. These examples show how a few bad choices can have a huge impact on an entire organization.

When Michael Vick was chosen by the Atlanta Falcons as the number-one overall pick in the 2001 NFL draft, almost everyone in the city was excited. Vick quickly became the starting quarterback and showed moves and speed that excited everyone in the league. The games sold out and endorsements were rolling in. The owner, Arthur Blank, awarded Vick a $130 million contract, and the excitement continued. After Blank hired a new head coach and made some key player personnel moves, everyone was looking forward to what might have been a super season. However, one afternoon in July of 2007, as I was fighting traffic on I-285, word came over the radio that Michael Vick and three others had been indicted on dogfighting charges. The news came as a shock to most people, even though it was already public knowledge that the federal government was investigating property owned by Vick. The league barred him from training camp, and most of his sponsors have dropped him. The nature of the alleged charges struck a nerve with a lot of people. I certainly hoped the charges were not true, but this situation shows the swiftness with which people will distance themselves when they suspect character issues.

Vick has now pleaded guilty to most of the charges against him and has been suspended from the NFL indefinitely. Even a star athlete with one of the largest contracts in the league can fall down without a solid foundation. Many people assume that good character comes along with great talent, but as this case clearly indicates, you must build a solid foundation of good character to help you maintain the gains you make by applying your talents. Character flaws are not always visible at first, but money and exposure will eventually bring them out. This is yet another example of how character affects everyone around you and therefore should be given much more thoughtful consideration.

Your character begins to develop at an early age. Your parents, teachers, and friends are most influential in the early years as you learn right from wrong.

You learn how to treat other people as you interact with your friends. As you get older and gain more exposure, your character will be challenged more frequently. You will no longer be under the watchful eye of your parents as you grow older and begin to make choices about how to live your life. This is a critical time to begin deciding what kind of person you want to be. You will also decide on the type of people that you want to associate with. Just remember, you will have to live with the choices you make.

I grew up with my grandparents, who were very strict and believed in attending church on a regular basis. They believed in the Ten Commandments and the Golden Rule. My two brothers and I were required to attend church and were expected to actively participate. If we were caught doing or saying something wrong, we were punished on the spot and without question. I remember once we stayed out past our curfew, and we tried to sneak in at 2:00 AM. Our grandmother, Katie, made us sit up in straight-backed chairs for the remainder of the night. She never let a bad deed go unpunished. She also had lots of help in monitoring our activities. Every parent or grandparent in the community would either turn you in or administer their own discipline. These were early lessons in being accountable for my actions.

My faith in God has helped me get through many difficult situations in both my personal and professional lives. Each of us, regardless of our profession, will face situations that we are not fully prepared to handle. I believe that our faith is tested through the challenges we face on a daily basis. Whenever I was unsure about what to do, I would spend some quiet time and listen for a signal from God. Sometimes when everyone else is trying to give you their opinion, you have to break away in order to hear what God would have you do in a given situation. You will find the strength to do the right thing in every situation you face. You may not get the outcome that you want, but you will get the outcome that is best. Think deeply before you make key life decisions.

Early in my career I sought some advice from Sam Travis, an executive at AT&T. I wanted to know what to expect as a new manager on the staff. His advice to me was that I should focus on building a reputation for good character, and that reputation would follow me around. His point was that in addition to performing well, you have to build relationships and demonstrate your character to others, so they have a good sense of who you really are. People are chosen for positions based on both their talent and character.

One of my role models for character was Frank D'Amelio, chief administrative officer and senior executive vice president for Alcatel-Lucent. Frank and I met in 1991 while we were both business unit controllers at AT&T. One of the first things I noticed about him was that he was very focused. He knew exactly what he wanted and had the discipline to make it happen. We were colleagues again later in another division of the company that would later become Lucent Technologies. In that assignment our responsibilities overlapped in the international arena. This is when I learned how strongly he believes in accountability. I was not holding our international colleagues accountable for implementing a new system, and Frank was upset with me. Part of the issue was my apprehension about dealing with people outside of the country. This all changed two years later, when I was given direct responsibility for financial operations in Latin America and Asia/Pacific. This was the beginning of my international travel, which took me to fourteen different countries. I will discuss the value of building those relationships in a later chapter.

Frank and I later attended executive education together at Columbia University in New York and had an opportunity to share our aspirations and values. It was during this time that I learned of his high integrity and how he stood out among the executives for his beliefs, values, and commitment to others. He always kept his commitments and always sought the truth in every situation, no matter who would get embarrassed. I admire that about him. The other thing that I admire about Frank is that, to this day, he is down-to-earth and still responds to my emails, even though I left the company eight years ago.

People define character in different ways, but generally it means your honesty, integrity, courage, and identity. It has also been defined as the sum of all of your behaviors. People will question your character when there is a gap between how you act and how you represent yourself to others. When someone has a bad experience dealing with you, they are less likely to want you in their inner circle in the future. This can lead to your being cut off from important communication channels or being passed over for a promotion.

When you decide on a new job, one important consideration should be the character of the new boss. Early in my career, I had a habit of giving each new boss the benefit of the doubt. What I learned very quickly is that a boss's character *does* matter. You want to make sure that he or she has integrity and will be open, honest, and fair. While I had a couple who were questionable, most of my bosses were of good character. The boss who I admired most was Steve Carson. While some feared him, I admired his strength and integrity. You knew what to expect and you always knew he had your back. Steve had a special way of making each of us feel valued. He was very clear about his expectations, and he held everyone accountable. There was a special kind of order among his team that was seldom seen in other organizations. Even with his direct style, he had a great sense of humor. This helped to ease the tension when things were not going well.

In addition to having a boss with good character, you should screen the people you inherit or select for your team. They too can make a huge difference in how successful you are and how you are perceived by others. I was fortunate during my career to have people who were hard-working, were loyal, and had good character. However, there was at least one case in which I actually had to take a sensitive project away from a manager and give it to someone else after I lost confidence in the manager. When I was a factory controller in Dallas, Texas, Ed Robertson, the general manager, asked me to oversee the human resources department until he could find a replacement for one of my peers, who had recently retired. Shortly after taking the assignment, there was a downturn in business, and we had to have a layoff. I asked the human resources manager—I will call her Sara—to handle the project, giving specific instructions on how many employees had to be laid off and how the process should work. When Sara presented the plan to me, I asked her if she had followed the procedures and whether there was anything in the plan that I needed to be concerned about. She told me that there was not. However, after reviewing the plan on my flight to Phoenix, I found several inconsistencies. I called back to the office and requested that the layoffs be put on hold until my concerns could be resolved. Sara attempted to proceed with the layoffs in my absence. When I returned from my trip two days later and saw what had happened, I took the project away from her and assigned it to two other managers in whom I had trust.

Sara then called the corporate vice president of human resources and told him that I had given the project to someone else and she was concerned about whether it would be done right. I received a call from the corporate executive, and I explained why I had assigned the project to someone else and how we were proceeding. Homer Johnson and Jim Staman, the two managers to whom I had made the assignment, were present for the call. The executive requested a copy of our revised plan. After a few days of review, he called me back and said that he didn't find any problems with our revised plan and only requested one minor change. I knew then that I had done the right thing.

When making tough decisions, I first review all of the facts and determine what legal and ethical options are available. Then I review the potential impact on stakeholders. I also ask myself if I would make the same decision if I were presented with the same set of facts in the future. If the answer is yes, I usually go with it. If the answer is no, then I don't do it. However, sometimes there are no good answers and you have to choose the lesser of two evils and try to make the best of it. This is why proper planning is so important. You can anticipate and avoid such difficult situations.

Whenever I consider whether to get involved in a transaction of any kind, I ask myself if I could live with the outcome should it ever see the light of day. You never want to depend on the darkness of night to protect you from your bad choices. Make your decisions as if the world is watching, because in many cases the world *is* watching. By taking these steps, you should be able to live with your decisions and defend them to others if that becomes necessary at a future date.

I have often preached about the wise use of power. Power and access should not be used for personal gain or inappropriate favors for others. A personnel assistant once withheld some information that may have affected my decision on a promotion. In order to help a friend, the personnel assistant withheld the fact that the person up for promotion had failed to get the review committee's approval. I approved the promotion after being told that everything was in order. The next day, Don Myhrberg, a division manager, came to my office and expressed his concern that I had approved a promotion that had failed the review committee. I asked the personnel assistant if she was aware of this when she requested my approval. I was surprised when she said yes, and I reminded her of my "wise use of power" speech, which she had heard before. I told her that I was disappointed in her actions and questioned whether I could trust her in the future. I think she finally got it.

I read an article in the *Atlanta Journal-Constitution* about a deputy who was sentenced to fifteen months in prison for accepting ten thousand dollars from a financial advisor who was seeking business from the sheriff's office. Whether it is cash or some other favor, personal gain in connection with your official duties is always a question of ethics or law. I remember when I was a young manager taking over the duties of night administrator at a company factory. The first day on the job, a train delivering materials broke a switch on the back of the building, and the conductor was concerned about losing his job. He said he was willing to pay me for the switch if I agreed not to report it. I immediately told him that I would not accept any money, but I would make a couple of phone calls and determine what the appropriate course of action should be. The conductor called me a short time later and apologized for putting me on the spot. I reported the incident to top management as the guidelines specified. This was a win-win outcome, because if I had gone along with the conductor's proposal we both would have lost our jobs. I think he realized that and decided to apologize. The more responsibility you have, the more valuable a good character foundation will be.

Most employers today require two or three character references. To protect themselves, many check the character references even before they make you an offer. Make sure that your good education and work experience are supported by a solid foundation of good character. Some people believe that what you do on your personal time should not affect your career and should not be anyone else's business. However, your credit rating, legal status, and organizational affiliations are all subject to review by your employer. As a matter of fact, insurance companies use credit ratings to determine the rates they charge for automobile insurance. With access to the Internet, companies are able to do background checks on job applicants, and apartment managers can do so as well. They can deny you access to an apartment if your credit is bad or you have a criminal record. These are personal matters that can affect your relationship with your employer.

If you own a business, you have to be concerned about the same kinds of issues. Customers, suppliers, investors, and employees will all expect you to be trustworthy and easy to do business with. They may not have as much access to your records, but they rely heavily on word of mouth. Your reputation will be a key driving force in the success of your business. As the owner you will have to decide what you want the company reputation to be and make sure your associates conduct themselves in accordance with your beliefs. The character of your business is the sum of your own character and that of your associates.

Companies usually have a written code of ethics that is strictly enforced. People enter the workforce from a variety of backgrounds, and it is the responsibility of management to protect the company's assets and reputation. Employees who violate the rules are usually dealt with very swiftly, as others observe the importance placed on maintaining good ethics. If you are unsure about a new employer's code of ethics, you should request a copy and become very familiar with it. You will be expected to abide by it and to ensure that your team does so as well.

From a personal perspective, you should make it a habit to always do the right thing, whether it is specifically mentioned in the code or not. Your reputation is valuable to you. There are many smart people in the world, but they don't all have great reputations. What you lack in knowledge can be made up for by a great reputation for honesty, integrity, and keeping your commitments. Our schools don't place enough emphasis on the value of a good reputation and how easily it can be destroyed. Whatever your personal vision happens to be, make sure you have built a solid foundation that will hold up when the going gets tough. A great vision will collapse on a weak foundation.

Practice Laying a Solid Foundation

To hold the gains you will make in life and earn the respect and trust of others, people have to know who you are and what you stand for. List the principles that define who you are and to what you are committed. They should represent rules that guide your life and your decision making. I know the development of my values was influenced partly by my grandparents. Reflecting on the sources of your own values can be helpful.

Principles that guide my life:

1.

2.

3.

4.

5.

6.

7.

8.

9.

10.

$$=== 5 ===$$

CHOOSING THE RIGHT PRIORITIES

Once you have decided what you want to do with your life and have laid a solid foundation, you should set priorities consistent with your vision and values. There aren't enough hours in the day to do everything that you might consider. Consequently, you will have to prioritize your activities to ensure you are getting the most important things done. Peter Drucker describes the effective executive as one who gets the right things done. Whether you are an executive, doctor, professor, or business owner, getting the right things done will be very important to your success.

Shirley Franklin had some very difficult decisions to make when she became mayor of Atlanta. She had to balance the city budget, clean up a scandal from the previous administration, and seek funding for a deteriorating sewer system. Mayor Franklin knew these were difficult and unpopular decisions, but she also knew that they had to be made to get the city back where it needed to be. We set priorities in our personal lives every day, but they don't necessarily require the support and commitment of others. In our professional lives, every decision we make will be scrutinized and challenged by those who may be impacted. If you have done your due diligence, you should be able to make a compelling case for why you are making a decision, but sometimes you will have to go with your gut and do what you think is right. Leaders must be courageous.

Herman J. Russell, owner and retired CEO of H.J. Russell & Company, knew that establishing himself as creditworthy was a critical first step in getting the money he needed to expand his business. He grew up poor and recognized very early the value of a dollar. He kept good records and paid his bills on time. His financial statements were kept in good shape, reflecting how he valued his business. He was getting the right things done. He was exercising personal leadership. His firm became the largest minority-owned business in Atlanta. He recently turned the CEO job over to his son.

When Jack Welch took over as CEO of GE, he knew the company had to change to remain competitive. Over the next several years he transformed GE from a highly industrial company to a diversified company, focused on being number one or two in each of its businesses. In order to do this, he had to set some priorities and make some difficult decisions. He and his top management team decided which businesses the company would be in and which ones it would eliminate. Getting out of some businesses required large layoffs, and getting into other businesses required some strategic hiring. Welch believed in developing his own leaders from within, so setting up a leadership development center was a high priority. Welch spent a lot of time at the center because he believed it was a great investment of time. GE executives have been highly sought after for important positions at many major corporations. Making leadership development a high priority was paying huge dividends.

My personal priorities were (and still are) faith, family, career, financial independence, and helping others. A good career would allow me to meet my family's financial needs and position me to help other people. I always discussed potential job changes with my wife and son prior to accepting them. Keeping my family together and happy was a high priority for me. Any job change would mean a new job for my wife and a new school for our son. My wife and son were very supportive of me and were willing to make the changes that were necessary for us to move ahead as a family.

When I was thirty-five, I made a strategic decision with my family's support to retire from my corporate career at the age of fifty. By making this decision fifteen years early, I was able to make plans for my second career and position myself to be financially able to walk away and know that my family's future was secure. This was a major priority for me, and through the grace of God I was able to make it happen. My wife chose to join me in retirement two years later. We are both teaching at Tuskegee University.

After making the tough decisions, it is important to follow through. One of the critical priorities in any profession is practice. Even people with lots of talent have to practice. I used to think that natural ability was all that was necessary for people to be successful. What I learned is that a person's performance is not only the result of natural ability but the result of countless hours of practice. Every professional has to practice good and correct techniques in order to stay at the top of their profession. If you do not have the level of success in your profession that you desire, take a look at the people who are the experts in your field, and you will find that they practice a lot harder than most. They know that practice has to be a priority in order to be at the top of any profession.

Gaining and maintaining professional competence is expected of all professionals. Preparing yourself to be the best at what you do should be a high priority. Professional competence will attract new relationships and new business. People love doing business with professionals they trust. They are motivated to spread the word about you and your ability to get things done. Whenever you are seeking a new doctor, dentist, or accountant, you usually do some research on who is out there and what their credentials are. However, before you make a final decision you usually ask a friend, relative, or coworker for a recommendation. They will share with you their perception of the competence and reputation of the professional that they use. Word of mouth is a powerful force, and you can use it to your advantage by making professional competence a priority.

An old African proverb says a lion has to get up early and start running in order to catch the slowest gazelle. Otherwise, he might not eat that day. A gazelle has to get up running to avoid being eaten by the lion, so they both have good reasons to get up running. However, it seems to me that the gazelle has a greater reason to get up running. If the lion gets up late, he simply misses a meal. On the other hand, if the gazelle gets up late, he becomes a meal. As a matter of fact, I believe that the gazelle should know where the lion is before he goes to sleep at night. I have that same belief about how to survive in business. You have to think like a gazelle and know where your competitors are before you go to sleep at night. This is especially true if your competitors have more resources and capabilities than you. Otherwise, they will eat you alive.

Practice Choosing the Right Priorities

Success is not about getting *everything* done. It is about getting the *right* things done. You have to decide what the right things are for you. Someone may help you decide what your job priorities are, but the priorities of your personal life and your career are yours to determine for yourself.

List your five most important priorities in each area below:

Personal priorities

1.

2.

3.

4.

5.

Professional priorities

1.

2.

3.

4.

5.

6

EMBRACING CHANGE

Change is necessary for both personal and professional growth. The rate of change in the world has increased significantly over time. Better and faster airlines have made global travel much more available to the average person. Newer technologies have improved communication and made information much more accessible. The result is a shift in how and where work is performed. During the '80s and '90s many manufacturing jobs were taken offshore because of lower labor rates in foreign countries. Today many technical and professional jobs have been outsourced to other countries. Companies are changing in order to compete in this environment. They are changing how they perform their work and where their work is performed. By making these changes, companies can move closer to their customers and offer more competitive prices. As companies change, their workforces must change as well. Workers are required to relocate or change the type of work they do. They will have to learn new technologies and travel to places they had never considered.

During the 1970s, many companies that were based in the Northeast and Midwest began moving their operations to the Southeast and Southwest. I joined Western Electric in 1973, shortly after it moved its cable operations from Buffalo to Atlanta. When I left Atlanta for New Jersey in 1982, the company was changing from copper cable to fiber-optics, which required an entirely new manufacturing process. By 1984, I was the controller at a factory in Dallas, Texas, where the entire facility, which made switching equipment, was being changed over to make energy systems and power supplies. The result was that many people had to relocate or change the type of work they were doing.

Embracing change requires us to let go of the past and create something new. This will involve training, taking risks, and being open to new ways of doing things. The problem we had in Dallas was that many employees had built their careers under the old system and were unsure how they would fare making something entirely new. Pride is a wonderful thing, but it can hold you back if you are unwilling to accept a new system, because it forces you to learn again. It took nearly a year and many false starts before we gained traction in making energy systems and power supplies. We had to make and celebrate small gains to get everyone pulling together toward our new future. Each person had to decide what personal change they were willing to make for the good of the organization.

Tom DeMaria, corporate vice president, was responsible for three of my career moves that involved significant change. He initially transferred me from Dallas to New Jersey to become the district manager of financial systems. This was a brand new area for me and really caused me to stretch my abilities. In this job I was responsible for the manufacturing cost systems and several cost databases that supported the pricing organization. Just as I was about to gain traction, Tom offered me a promotion to corporate accounting. The offer came just two weeks after I had been told that my group would be relocating to Atlanta. I turned the offer down, and we had a discussion about the implications of turning down a promotion. He made it clear that I had to be more flexible in the future. About three months later I was promoted and transferred to Atlanta. I became division manager for one of the company's two financial operations centers. The financial operations centers were responsible for transaction processing for payroll, accounts payable, customer billing, receivables, and inventories. After being on that assignment for about a year and a half, and only a week after being assured I wouldn't have to move anytime soon, I was told that a "great opportunity" had opened up in New Jersey and it would give me some experience on the service side of AT&T.

I became the controller for the consumer long distance business unit, which was the largest in the company at that time. This meant a change from measuring products to measuring minutes. Minutes represented the heart and soul of the long distance business. My new boss was Tom Brown, a very hands-on guy who never felt he had enough details. It was a struggle for me at first because he was so different from Tom DeMaria in the level of detail that he required. I had to learn the new systems and processes and quickly build new relationships in order to be effective. There was no turning back. I had to find a way to be successful in this new environment. I give DeMaria credit for pushing me to broaden my perspective and my experience base. Before long I learned how to be effective in the new environment. My previous experience had prepared me to embrace the change and move on.

Whatever your profession happens to be, you can bet there will be change. You will change as an individual when you are exposed to new people and new methods of getting things done. Change is usually good for self-development. You are required to think more and adapt to different situations. Change will challenge you and cause you to stretch beyond your comfort zone. I remember when I received my first promotion to supervisor of cost accounting. It was totally unexpected, since I had never worked in the cost accounting department. I even asked my manager if the company was trying to set me up for failure. He assured me that if I did the job well, I would be just fine. This was a major departure from my comfort zone. It was an opportunity to grow and learn more about the company. Little did I know that most of my future assignments would be in areas where I had never worked. The assignments forced me to learn more and to develop my social skills, as I had to meet and supervise new people all the time. There were changes in processes, systems, and locations with every move. By embracing change I was able to grow and develop my leadership skills.

When you look at the backgrounds of highly successful people, you will often find that they had to relocate to different cities in order to match their skills with opportunities. Talented people sometimes wait for opportunities to come to them. Sometimes it happens, but more often than not, they have to move to where the opportunities are. Johnny Carson grew up in Nebraska but had to move to New York and California to live out his dream. Oprah Winfrey was born in Mississippi and found her fame and fortune in Chicago after a brief stay in Baltimore. Robin Roberts of *Good Morning America* grew up in Mississippi and lived in Atlanta for a while before moving on to New York. In addition to transforming yourself, you may have to move to where the action is if there are no good opportunities in your hometown.

Change is such a big part of growth. When you change jobs or careers you will have to develop new relationships. When you get a new boss or become a new boss you will likely experience change. You may even decide to change your profession. Being proactive and deciding how to deal with change is a better strategy than constantly reacting to change or resisting it. When I was offered a chance to transfer to company headquarters in New Jersey, my initial response was "no way." I didn't want to deal with all the change that would be involved. As a matter of fact, even after I finally decided to go, I was still not fully embracing the change. A salesman stopped by my home and tried to sell me a water-purification system, and I told him I didn't need one because I was counting the days until I left. He said, "That is a lousy way to live. You should enjoy it while you are here and make the most of it. You should embrace the change."

After that first relocation my family and I learned how to embrace the changes that came over the next several years. We moved to Dallas next and then back to New Jersey four years later. From there we moved to Atlanta before returning to New Jersey for the third time. Fortunately, we had learned to embrace change, because each move meant new positions for both my wife and me and a new school for our son. We always discussed the moves before deciding to take them, but once we were there we made the best of it. Each of us developed lasting relationships, learned about different lifestyles, and sharpened our skills by taking on new challenges.

During the course of my long career I had to manage large groups of people: technical and nontechnical, domestic and international, union and nonunion. I worked the day shift, the evening shift, and the night shift. I spent time in manufacturing and in services. I worked in finance, systems, and human resources and had seventeen different bosses. Embracing change was what allowed me to take on these challenges and learn from each new job. Just working for a large company like AT&T required a certain tolerance for change. Those who embraced it were able to learn and develop new skills. There will not be training manuals for dealing with every situation. Therefore, the ability to learn from mistakes and the forces of change will be critical. You must learn to lead yourself through change so that you can effectively lead others through it.

Earlier, I mentioned having to take on leadership roles in many unfamiliar areas. New leaders are seldom given an agenda or specific job-related training. They have to teach themselves through asking good questions, observation, and trial and error. They develop their own agendas after learning what the stakeholders' issues are. No one but yourself will lead you through this process. After you have gone through the process a few times you know what to expect at each step along the way. Your method of learning may be different from others, so you will have to determine what works for you. When you are able to learn assignments quickly and get results you become a candidate for larger assignments.

Often people resist change because they fear the unknown. If they have done well on a job or in a business, the thought of change brings discomfort. "Will I fare as well on the new job or in the new business?" To increase your confidence, you have to look at your previous success in making changes and that of others who have also changed. Understand why you are changing, what is involved, and what the main factors of success are. Change at any level requires leadership. You must understand the goal, believe in it, and lead yourself through the change. You have to convince yourself first before you can convince others of the benefits of a change. You will have to share your vision of the business after the change is made and show others how they fit in. When people know how they will fit in the new business, they are more likely to participate in making change happen.

Practice Embracing Change

Change is an inevitable part of life, and we can ignore it, fight it, or embrace it. To ignore it is to be left behind, and to fight it requires a lot of energy and resources. By embracing change you will learn and grow, as it will challenge you to think and act differently.

List three significant changes in your life and describe how you dealt with each. How will you deal with them in the future?

1.

2.

3.

7

OVERCOMING ADVERSITY

We have all had to deal with adversity at some point in our lives. It may have been a job loss, a divorce, or the loss of a loved one. It could also be a bad boss, lost job opportunity, or financial difficulties. Some learning usually results from adversity, as it deepens your thinking, changes your perspective, and helps you appreciate the good times even more. When I was growing up I thought it was unfair that I had to live with my grandparents while most of my friends had their parents at home with them and seemed to have money to spend and opportunities to go places. My grandparents did not have much, but they believed in hard work, honesty, and responsibility. I learned how to become self-reliant, respect others, and be accountable for my actions. As a result, when I entered college it didn't bother me that I had to work to pay for my room and board. That was consistent with the way my grandparents had raised me. I was able to celebrate by myself when my family members could not attend my graduation.

Whether your childhood was filled with memorable days or doses of adversity, you will have to deal with adversity at some point in your life. When that day arrives it is important to remember that it is not what happens to you in life that determines your destiny but rather how you respond to what happens. You have the ability to choose your response after assessing the situation and determining what your best response should be. You can condition yourself to handle adversity in the best possible way. We take a lot for granted until things suddenly don't go our way. As we learn to anticipate the possibilities in life and how to cope, we are also strengthening our ability to deal effectively with future adversity. According to Bill George, author of *True North: Discover Your Authentic Self* (2007), the hardest person you will ever have to lead is yourself.

Michael Jordan was cut from his high school basketball team. Most people would have given up at that point, but he used the event to learn more about himself, his practice habits, and the game of basketball. He learned from his teammates and coaches and went on to be a star at the University of North Carolina. Michael was drafted by the Chicago Bulls and became one of the best players in the game. He never stopped learning, and he never stopped practicing. He was the star of six NBA championship teams. His career was temporarily interrupted when his father was killed by two young men who found him asleep in his car. Michael tried his hand at baseball, but it didn't work out, so he returned to basketball and finished his career. His desire to be the best and his willingness to lead himself through some tough challenges speak volumes about his character.

Lee Iacocca was fired by Ford Motor Company before being hired to save the Chrysler Corporation from bankruptcy. It was totally unexpected, and he was greatly disappointed, but he had learned from his father that you never give up. He convinced the government to extend Chrysler a loan and led it back to profitability. Several new car brands were introduced on his watch, and he became one of the most respected people in the industry during his time. Many even wanted him to run for president of the United States, but he declined. He recently published a book titled *Where Have All the Leaders Gone?* (2007). In the book he talks about how our government and business leaders have lost the courage to make bold moves and deal with the difficult issues of our day. He urges voters to hold our politicians accountable and to be more active in their communities. Leaders who have not learned how to lead themselves have difficulty leading others, since leadership is largely by example. Leaders who do not have experience dealing with adversity or don't have a history of making and keeping commitments will find it hard to inspire those traits in others.

A big motivator for me was when someone told me that I couldn't do something. Since I was black, poor, and attending a small college, it was pretty common in the early days for people to underestimate me. A gentleman from a major corporation interviewed me during my junior year in college and suggested that I could not make the same grades at a major college. I disagreed with him, and I decided to take classes at the University of Michigan that fall to prove my point. I received the same grade point average at Michigan that I had received at Tuskegee. There may have been a few students at Tuskegee who couldn't make it at Michigan, but I didn't think I was one of them. I was determined to prove it to him and to myself.

That same determination drove me to take on some difficult assignments during my career. There were two jobs in particular that I was forewarned about, and they really were filled with adversity. The first one came about when our vice president, John Hahn, asked me what I thought the problem was at our Dallas factory. I told him I believed it was a financial leadership problem. He came back a few days later and asked me to transfer to Dallas to become the new factory controller. My new boss did not like the fact that I was coming, and my new peers were not excited either. They questioned my motives, my youth, my experience, and my ability to relate to them. I was accused of leaking information to the corporate office, among other things, and my performance appraisal was reduced by two levels. Most people would have looked for a way out, but I was determined to show my abilities and convince my leader that I was on his side. It took me almost two years, but I earned my leader's respect, and my appraisal was restored to the original level. I was also able to gain the respect of my peers. Things were going pretty well when I left for New Jersey two years later.

The second assignment filled with adversity came later in my career, when two of my former bosses warned me not to take an assignment. The position was chief financial officer for AT&T's Information Management Services Division. The day of my promotion, Pam Dage, the division controller, called me and said she was planning to leave. She had been a candidate for the CFO job. There was infighting among my new peers, and the unit was running a significant financial loss and had not been straightforward with top management about the problem. Again, I thought I could make a difference by getting the right people talking to each other and agreeing on some priorities. You have to be able to get enough people willing to do the right thing. Because I would not go along with the previous program of denial, I was sometimes not invited to certain meetings. As the problems got worse, my boss and I had several meetings with Alex Mandl, president and chief operating officer of AT&T at the time. I will never forget our last meeting in Mandl's office. He got so upset with my boss that he walked out and left us sitting there.

This situation came to an end a few months later, when Ron Ponder, a former Sprint executive, was hired as senior vice president, reporting to Mandl. Ponder came in and began asking questions. At first my boss tried to answer all of the questions himself, but Ponder was a pretty smart guy. He began calling us at home to get a better understanding of what was going on. He sized up the situation and soon began to "clean house." Most of the top-level executives were either reassigned or forced out.

I was transferred to an assignment in another division after meeting with AT&T's chief financial officer, Rick Miller. Rick wanted to know what had happened, what I had learned from the assignment, and why I was the right person for my next assignment. It was the longest interview I had ever had. An hour and a half later we shook hands and I was off to my new assignment. Some of the things I learned: always listen to wise counsel, check out your new boss and the group culture in advance, and speak up as soon as you become aware that something is wrong.

The job that I was transferred to was challenging but also familiar. I was the financial vice president of operations and systems, reporting to Steve Carson, chief financial officer of network systems. I was responsible for network systems' transaction processing and financial systems. Network systems was organized into both product and customer business units. One of my responsibilities was to oversee the design of a financial reporting system and a new schedule of authorizations to support the new structure. This was familiar territory, since I had previously worked in financial operations and systems. When Lucent Technologies was spun off from AT&T, this job was expanded to include similar functions for all of Lucent's operations in the United States, Latin America, and Asia. Adversity had yet again led to new learning opportunities.

Shortly after Lucent Technologies was formed, Michael Montemarano, financial vice president, and I were challenged to consolidate all of the company's accounting operations around the globe into ten financial hubs. This was being done to reduce costs and facilitate the implementation of a new financial system called SAP. I was responsible for Latin America and Asia/Pacific. Michael was responsible for Europe, the Middle East, and Africa. I had a series of meetings with the managers in Latin America and Asia and reviewed several proposals before finally deciding to set up hubs in Mexico City, Sao Paulo, Beijing, and Singapore. After their establishment, most of my international travel was to those cities, even though we continued to maintain some operations in Buenos Aires, Argentina, and Hong Kong.

Most of my international trips were safe and uneventful; however, I once went to a hospital in Mexico City while traveling there alone. I was in Mexico City to get a progress report on the hub formation that I mentioned earlier. I didn't know at the time how serious my blood pressure problem had become. After my Mexican colleagues noticed that I was not feeling well they called a company doctor, who took one look at my pressure and recommended that I go to a hospital as soon as possible. My first reaction was to take the next flight back to the United States, but my Mexican colleagues were able to persuade me to go to the hospital. I didn't tell my wife or my boss until the next day because I felt there was little that they could do, and I didn't want them to panic. It is hard to help someone under those conditions. I stayed at the hospital several hours until my blood pressure came down and then returned to my hotel. My team was waiting for me to join them for dinner, but I declined. They gave me a nice gift for visiting them, and I turned in for the evening. I called my wife and my boss the next morning and told them what had happened. I left Mexico soon afterward.

With all the pressure of global responsibility, things around my office in Alpharetta, Georgia, were beginning to heat up. Late one afternoon I received a call from Gil Harris, vice president of auditing and security, asking about my safety around the office. I was quite surprised and began asking questions about why he had concerns. He explained that my boss, Jim Lusk, had received some calls from Alpharetta and had reason to believe that my safety was in jeopardy. I felt like it was an overreaction, but I went along with the plan. Gil sent one of his security officers to inspect my office and my home, which was a few miles away. The security officer recommended that glass doors be installed at the entrance to the waiting area outside of my office and that I have a new security system installed at my home. Many people would have been intimidated by this situation, but I didn't let it affect my professional life. I had an open-door policy, and I spoke freely to anyone who wanted to talk to me. Therefore, I concluded that this was a scare tactic to influence the difficult decisions that had been made regarding two recent terminations. My guess is that one of the employees called my boss after the incident. He never explained the reason for his actions. I assume he had concern for my safety.

It would have been easy to blame the incident on racism since the majority of the organization was white and the two people terminated were white, but I made it a policy to never play the race card. I believed I could perform well enough to hold my own with anybody, so I spent my time focusing on ways to get better at what I was doing. You have to tune some things out, because you can easily slip into a victim mentality. That is not where I wanted to be. You should always focus on becoming the very best at what you do and being a role model for how to treat people. Your actions will speak volumes to those who attempt to undermine you or deal with you on a different level.

Earlier in my career, I was faced with a crisis involving this same organization. About two hundred employees had been promised pay protection while a new pay plan was being implemented. After the workers organized and joined a union, they were told that the pay protection was no longer valid. This happened shortly before I took over the job. One of the employees brought it to my attention, and I took time to verify the facts. What had happened was that management became embarrassed and ticked off about the employees organizing a union. Therefore, people were told that all bets were off for pay protection. It was against my values to renege on a promise, and it was now my responsibility to decide what to do. My bosses were initially against any consideration for the group, but after the group wrote a letter to the CEO they became more supportive, and I was allowed to pursue the honoring of the initial pay protection agreement. It saved employees over three hundred dollars per month and over six hundred dollars where couples were involved. When we learned that the pay-protection package had been approved, the affected employees wrote me a nice thank-you letter. I felt like I had done the right thing.

A good leader is one who stays calm in the face of adversity. You should assess the situation and get all of the facts before deciding on a course of action. Your team will expect you to be fair, objective, and willing to listen. What everyone should get from the experience is new knowledge about how things can be done better in the future. You and everyone on your team should seek to do things differently. Adversity, if handled properly, can be a great learning experience for everyone.

Practice Overcoming Adversity

Just as change is inevitable, adversity also shows up at some point in everyone's lives. You have probably heard the statement "God won't give me anything I cannot handle." Overcoming adversity builds strength and character.

Describe a time in your life when you had to overcome adversity.

What steps did you take?

What did you learn about yourself?

How did it make you feel?

8

BUILDING RELATIONSHIPS

No one succeeds alone. No matter what your profession, you will need to establish and maintain good, positive relationships to be successful. There are relationships with clients, colleagues, suppliers, governments, and community leaders. Sometimes you will need expertise, and other times you will need access to information. The world we live in is highly interactive and interdependent. A leader's effectiveness is either enhanced or diminished by the quality of his or her relationships. A person who is unusually bright may underestimate the value of relationships, but people like to feel that they matter. The best way to convince them that they do matter is to include them and value their input. I have always believed in building relationships. I owe a great deal of my success to the cooperation and support of others.

Ann Mulcahy, CEO of Xerox, was asked if someone

noticed her and started moving her up in management. Her reply was, "It should never be just one person. It should be a series of relationships." Ms. Mulcahy took time to build relationships all around the company long before she became a candidate for CEO. When I reflect back on my own career I remember countless relationships resulting from relocations, working at headquarters, working on special projects, and international travel. Great relationships don't just happen; they take a lot of work. You have to be proactive, but you also have to be a good listener and willing to assist others first. Those relationships helped me because I was able to build a reputation throughout the financial community for having integrity, getting the right things done, and getting along with others.

Most leaders have done a good job of demonstrating their technical abilities early in their careers, since that is what most early assessments are based on. As you move up and take on additional responsibilities, you will be evaluated more on your people skills, since influence becomes your main method of getting things done. You will have to lead others who are, in many cases, smarter than you are. That is why many companies use 360-degree feedback instruments as a part of their leadership development programs. They want to measure your effectiveness working with and through others. Some argue that such measurements are subjective, but they play a critical role in the development process. People have actually lost jobs that they were technically qualified for because they failed in their relationships with others. Robert Nardelli, chairman and CEO of Home Depot, recently resigned because of the strained relationship he had with shareholders. He has now become CEO of Chrysler Corporation, which was purchased by a private investment group. Since Chrysler is privately owned, there are no shareholders to deal with.

Great relationships open up doors in both your personal and professional lives. People like to do business with people they know, so it is important to put yourself in a position to become known. You can seek high-profile assignments, make presentations to senior managers, or volunteer to lead a community service activity. Each of these efforts will give others an opportunity to get to know you better and assess your potential. You can even benefit from such exposure long after your career is over. After I retired from Lucent Technologies, I received three job offers within the first ninety days. Two of them resulted from my relationship with Ben Newhouse, who was dean of the College of Business at Tuskegee University. The third one was the result of a relationship with the president of a local university: I was given an opportunity to teach at the college level. A year later, while I was writing my first book, I contacted the editor of *Management Accounting Magazine* (now called *Strategic Finance Magazine*) to get permission to use an article in my book. The editor requested a copy of my book when it was completed and invited me to speak at the Institute of Management Accountants national conference in Nashville, Tennessee. Also, in 2005, I was invited to the South Regions Minority Business Council meeting in Birmingham, Alabama. I was scheduled to introduce Governor Bob Riley of Alabama at a luncheon meeting, which was attended by over three hundred people. When Governor Riley did not show up due to an emergency, I had an opportunity to speak in his place. I had only about twenty minutes to prepare, but it was the opportunity of a lifetime, and I just had to do it. As you can see, relationships lead to opportunities.

During my first teaching tour at Tuskegee University in 1999, Dr. Benjamin Newhouse, dean of the College of Business and Information Science, was planning an international trip for a small group of students. He asked me if my wife and I would be interested in going along as chaperones. The other reason he wanted me to go along was my business contacts in the region. Through my contacts in Singapore and Hong Kong we were able set up tours with five or six companies in the region to expose our students to the nature of international business. Sandy Welfare was our contact in Singapore. Sandy and I had worked together while I was with Lucent Technologies. I had sponsored her assignment to Singapore, and we had kept in touch since my retirement. Dan Lovatt was the contact in Hong Kong, and we also knew each other from Lucent. Dan had been in the region for several years and was able to arrange some very informative company visits, including dinner at a world-famous restaurant.

During the summer of 2004, my wife and I traveled to Beijing, China, for a week. The trip was part of an adult education program sponsored by a Chinese university. My assignment was to teach a two-day accounting class in exchange for the free trip. Dr. Benjamin Newhouse was again instrumental in setting this up. I spent several weeks preparing for the classes. I took a PowerPoint class to sharpen my presentation skills and brushed up on my accounting knowledge. Obtaining the class requirements in advance was somewhat difficult. As a result, I would have to modify my presentation once we arrived in China. I was not comfortable with the lack of information, but I had little choice. This was shaping up to be the opportunity of a lifetime, even though I had reservations at first.

When we arrived in Beijing, we were met by two men in a very small car. Our luggage was too large to fit in the trunk, so it had to be tied down to secure it. We traveled about four hours by car to a city in southeast China where the university was located. When we arrived, we were taken to a very nice hotel and assigned to a room on the twelfth floor. Minutes later, I received a phone call from our contact to come down to the eleventh floor for a meeting. When I walked into the room, I saw about five people standing around, who were quickly introduced. Some of them were from the university and others were from the Chinese government. They wanted me to make some changes to my presentation, which I had sent to them in advance. I had not seen their computer equipment yet, and they were already asking me to make changes. I took notes and requested to see the equipment as soon as possible. They suggested that I could use the business center at the hotel to make the changes. I would not see their computer equipment until the first day of class.

The university provided a translator for the classes, and he also served as our driver and guide for the two days we spent on the campus. The translator and I learned to work together very quickly. The sessions went very well, even though it was hot in the room and the computer went down several times each day. I was just as curious to see what was going to happen as they were. I had never imagined that I would travel that far into mainland China, let alone stand in front of seventy-five Chinese students teaching accounting through a translator. This was yet another example of the power of relationships. I cannot imagine setting up such a challenging and educational trip without the benefit of great relationships.

Since I had used translators before to manage my teams in Latin America, my first day in the classroom went pretty well. Once I was introduced, I shared with the class what a great opportunity this was for my wife and me to visit their country. I explained that my corporate career had been in accounting and it was a subject that I loved to talk about. The class was mostly mid-level managers with a few undergraduate students mixed in. The undergraduate students could speak English and would catch me during the breaks and ask questions about corporate careers. The adults in the class were more interested in accounting policy and the government's role in regulating corporations. They also requested a session on strategic planning and leadership. Making these changes kept me up pretty late that night, but I was ready to go when class resumed the next morning.

During the lunch break on the second day, a professor at the university offered to have one of his English-speaking students take my wife shopping. Rose loves to shop, but we had made an agreement that we would not become separated on this unusual trip. The professor was very persuasive, and we listened but declined the initial offer. He continued to assure us that it was safe and we would be reunited at the end of the afternoon. We reluctantly agreed. When I returned to the hotel that evening, Rose was there as they had promised. I found that you have to evaluate people wherever you are and decide if you can trust them. This group had proven to be trustworthy.

That night there was a dinner celebration to recognize the students and to thank my wife and me for coming. Several students from the class spoke about their experiences. The feedback was great. It was a very nice dinner and a great way to wrap up the program. It was well attended and quite a festive event. They must have toasted everything under the sun, but I had to bow out after the second drink. We were ready to get some rest, and we had to pack for our trip back to Beijing.

Back in Beijing, we visited the Great Wall, Tiananmen Square, and the Forbidden City. It was exciting to visit these attractions after hearing so much about them over the years. Our tour guides were very knowledgeable and did a great job explaining the history behind each attraction. We were so concerned about getting separated from them, since there were thousands of tourists at these attractions. One of the guides saw our concerned looks and said, "You don't have to worry about finding us. We can easily find you."

That evening we had a great dinner of Peking duck at a famous Beijing restaurant. The next day we were driven to the airport and assisted with our check-in before doing some last-minute shopping. I could only reflect with amazement on how this whole experience had come about. We had learned so much about how the Chinese people live in both major cities and in rural areas. We had visited their most popular tourist attractions without having to wait in long lines. This had been a great opportunity.

I called Dr. Newhouse to thank him for the wonderful opportunity and to give him some tips about what to expect, since he and his wife were making the same visit the next week. We have not had a chance to compare notes, but it had to be a once-in-a-lifetime trip for them as well. I am always grateful for opportunities presented to me, even when there is risk and challenge involved. My wife, Rose, is a real trouper when it comes to taking risks and traveling to new places.

Practice Building Relationships

No one succeeds alone, so you will need the cooperation and support of others. This is why you should
seek to build relationships at every opportunity. Those
with established relationships will move ahead much
sooner than those without.

*List five key relationships that you have already
established.*

1.

2.

3.

4.

5.

*List three new relationships that you will commit to
developing.*

1.

2.

3.

9

MAXIMIZING SYNERGY

Synergy exists when the whole is greater than the sum of its parts. The power of synergy allows you to multiply your effectiveness. Successful people understand how to use this power in every situation. You want to create win-win solutions and leverage your relationships. Companies often merge with each other on the belief that together they can deliver a better product or service than they could ever produce alone. Take a look at your current relationships and see what opportunities might exist to form a partnership on a project or business opportunity that will create synergy.

I talked earlier about personal leadership in the areas of ownership, character, courage, vision, and relationships. These are key areas in becoming the type of person that attracts others. Since few people possess all of these attributes, as a leader of yourself, you will need to recognize your gaps and partner with people who have complementary skills.

A person who is a strategic thinker and decision maker will likely need someone who is a good organizer of details. A person who is a generalist may need someone who has good technical skills. A technical person may need to find someone with excellent people skills. You want to create effectiveness through a partnership of complementary skills.

The more you know about the people around you, the better you can make use of their unique abilities. What you want to achieve is effectiveness, and having the ability to influence others is the key. You begin by listening to those around you to understand and appreciate their unique perspectives. I used this approach whenever I took on a new job. I got to know the boss, the team, and the clients. By listening closely to each of these stakeholders, I was able to learn and appreciate where the opportunities for synergy existed. By building trust, sharing information, and ultimately creating a vision that reflected their needs, I created synergy through their buy-in and support.

You have heard about teamwork all of your life: in school, in sports, and at work. Teamwork creates synergy, and the team with the most synergy usually wins. The New England Patriots didn't have a lot of superstars on their team when they won three Super Bowls in four years. They had a coach who knew how to maximize synergy. He designed a system in which every player on the field had an important role to play, and a significant part of that role was creating synergy with teammates.

The world we live in today is highly interdependent. We need the talents and skills of many other people to succeed. If you are a perfectionist, you may find it somewhat difficult to work on teams. The work of teams is to get it right, not to be right. A perfection-ist wants to be right all of the time, and that makes others feel less valued or not needed. A great team seeks contributions from all of its members, and the result is usually better than what any one member could achieve. Are you willing to share the spotlight for the good of the team?

Practice Maximizing Synergy

Synergy is the incremental value created when the parts of a whole work together. Creating synergy is a powerful way to increase your influence.

Describe a time when you created synergy and achieved an important goal.

List three new opportunities for synergy in your professional life.

1.

2.

3.

— 10 —

GIVING BACK

Giving back can be a powerful thing. Some people think that giving back means simply giving money to your favorite charities. To me, it means giving some of your time, wisdom, and wealth to the next generation. When you think about all the times that you were the beneficiary of someone's giving, it makes perfect sense to give back. When you have had a successful career, accumulating wisdom and wealth, there is no better way to spend the remainder of your life than sharing some of your blessings with others.

I can remember receiving help from my high school teachers, college professors, and corporate mentors. I was not always sure why they took an interest in me, but I later learned that it was their way of giving back. They didn't give back to everyone but gave to those who demonstrated potential and a willingness to learn. During my long corporate career, I learned that you must have sponsors, people willing to be an advocate for you. It was not as simple as asking someone to be your sponsor. You had to earn their sponsorship through your performance, character, and leadership. Investors invest in companies based on their confidence in the leadership. They continue to invest if the company delivers value. You have to give sponsors a reason to invest in you by performing at a high level. They will continue to invest in you if you continue to deliver.

Whenever I received a promotion or key assignment, I was determined to deliver the expected performance because I didn't want to lose my sponsors. They had invested in me, and I felt an obligation to live up to their expectations as well as my own. If you don't have a sponsor right now, you should expand your network. Examine whether you have given potential sponsors a reason to invest in you. No one wants to invest either time or money unless there is an excellent chance of positive returns.

I have talked to so many people who felt like everyone was just looking out for themselves and their close friends. I have always believed that if people are not knocking down your door with opportunities, there must be some room for improvement. It could be a lack of knowledge, experience, or something as simple as exposure. I listened whenever someone gave me feedback, even if I didn't like it. Feedback is the way to find out what you need to work on. I have learned that most people are willing to help you if you are willing to help yourself. They won't give you an opportunity, but they will help you earn one.

When I retired in 1999, I developed a plan for how I would spend my time. I wanted to teach at a university, do some leadership coaching, write a book, and learn to play golf. The first three "projects" were my way of giving back. I began teaching at Tuskegee University in 1999, before taking time off to write my first book. During that same time I started a leadership coaching practice. I returned to teaching in 2005, my second tour at Tuskegee University. I enjoy teaching students about the opportunities and challenges of life. My twenty-six years of business experience and world travel provide a unique perspective. I also coach business professionals on the behaviors that can make or break a career. Teaching and coaching provide excellent ways to impact the lives of others.

There are many different ways to give back. If you have a special skill that is needed in a given community or you have contacts or resources that could help meet a community's needs, you can volunteer a few hours a month and make a huge difference. Many organizations do fundraising for needy schoolchildren or homeless people. There is community work to maintain your community. All you have to do is look around you and see where you can make a difference. The great feeling you get from helping others is hard to match. You can use your influence to mobilize others for a good cause. You could paint schools, make home repairs for the elderly, or clean up the streets. My son is an accounting professor, and he provides free tax services during tax season. You too will find enjoyment by doing something good for others to express your gratitude for the great life you will have.

Everyone has something that they can give. If you start while you are young and get involved, you will find it much easier to transition at the end of your career. I remember taking my leadership team out at Christmastime to give gifts to kids at a local hospital. Another time I painted the inside of a school. It takes time to develop the habit of giving back to help others. We are so busy these days that helping others has to be a conscious decision and a part of our daily routine.

My goal in writing this book is to reveal the power of personal leadership and provide a roadmap for young adults or others seeking to enhance their careers. The main message is that you must take ownership of your future, create a personal vision of what you want to achieve, and develop the character and relationships to attract people who will help you realize your dreams. Leading yourself prepares you to lead others.

Practice Giving Back

Giving back is an important part of completing a life cycle. It is a way to continue the bond that holds us together as a society. Those who are fortunate enough to have received great blessings should show some appreciation by giving to those who are less fortunate. Think back to a time when you received support from others. Did you ever wonder why they helped you when there was nothing to gain in return? Think about it.

List three things that you have given to others in the past year.

1.

2.

3.

List five things that you are committed to give in the upcoming year.

1.

2.

3.

4.

5.

=11=

SUMMING IT UP

I promised to take you through the process of leading yourself. Leading yourself prepares you to lead others. The process begins only when you make the decision to take ownership of your future. With ownership comes accountability. Personal leadership is taking ownership of your future and holding yourself accountable for the choices you make and their consequences. Seeking to understand yourself and the world around you gives you the knowledge base to make better choices. Creating a vision gives focus to your desires and provides a pathway. With your vision in place it becomes important to lay a good foundation upon which to build your vision. Your foundation will consist of character, courage, values, and identity. Knowing who you are and what you believe gives you a basis for making difficult choices. Choosing the right priorities will help you get the right things done. Your energy will go toward the things that will have the biggest impact. Embracing change helps to reduce resistance and facilitates learning and growth. It will stretch you and help you develop your skills. Life can be filled with adversity, yet it provides a great learning opportunity. Your ability to overcome adversity will have a big impact on how far you go in the world. No one succeeds alone, so building and maintaining relationships will be critical. You should surround yourself with people who have skills that you don't have. You can create synergy when you engage your team in a way that uses everyone's ability. Giving back is a natural part of the process. It makes the other steps worthwhile. All of these steps are required to successfully lead oneself. By mastering them, you will be able to effectively lead others and make the most of every situation.

REFERENCES

Cook, Rhonda. 2007. Tearful ex-chief deputy sentenced. *The Atlanta Journal-Constitution*, August 9, 2007.

Covey, Stephen. 1989. *The Seven Habits of Highly Effective People*. New York: Simon & Schuster.

Drucker, Peter. 1999. *Management Challenges for the 21st Century*. New York: HarperCollins.

George, Bill. 2007. *True North*. San Francisco: Jossey-Bass.

Iacocca, Lee. 2007. *Where Have All the Leaders Gone?* New York: Scribner

Lanier, Danny. 2002. *Setting the Pace for Business Success*. Mt. Pleasant: Corinthian Books.

Mulling, Emory. 2002. *The Mulling Factor*. Bradenton: DC Press.

Paz-Frankel, Einat. 2007. Business Pulse results: Reputable college isn't enough to succeed in business. *Memphis Business Journal*, June 13, 2007.

Quinn, Robert. 1996. *Deep Change*. San Francisco: Jossey-Bass.

Stanley, Thomas. 2000. *The Millionaire Mind*. Kansas City: Andrew McMeel Publishing.

Welch, Jack. 2005. *Winning*. New York: HarperCollins.

INDEX

Index

N

Nardelli, Robert, 81
Newhouse, Ben, 81, 82, 83

O

ownership, personal, viii,
5–6, 101
author's experience,
2–4
examples, 1–2
worksheet, 7

P

personal leadership, vii–
ix, 101–102
personal reflection, value
of, 12
Ponder, Ron, 70
power, use/abuse, 40–42
practice, value of, 50
priority selection, viii, 101
author's experience,
49–50
examples, 47–49
and practice, 50
and professional
competence,
50–51
value of, 47, 48, 50–52
worksheet, 53–54
professional competence,
50–51

R

relationships, personal,
viii, 102

author's experience,
81–87
establishing, 80
examples, 79–80, 81
value of, 79, 80–81
worksheet, 88
reputation and character,
43–44
Richie, Lionel, 26–27
Roberts, Robin, 59–60
Rose, Pete, 31–32
Russell, Herman J., 48

S

self-understanding, viii,
101
examples of, 15–16
factors in, 9–14
worksheet, 18–19
Smith, Fred, 22–23
Smith, Jim, 15–16
Snow, Eric, 1–2
sponsors, 93–94
Stanley, Thomas J., 5
Stratford, Randy, 16
success factors, 4–5
synergy, viii, 102
defined, 89
examples of, 90–91
and teamwork, 90–91
value of, 89
in the workplace, 89–
90
worksheet, 92

T

talents, identifying, 9–10

107

Printed in the United States
111243LV00003B/19-114/P

9 781604 940411